My Body is
Special
and belongs to me

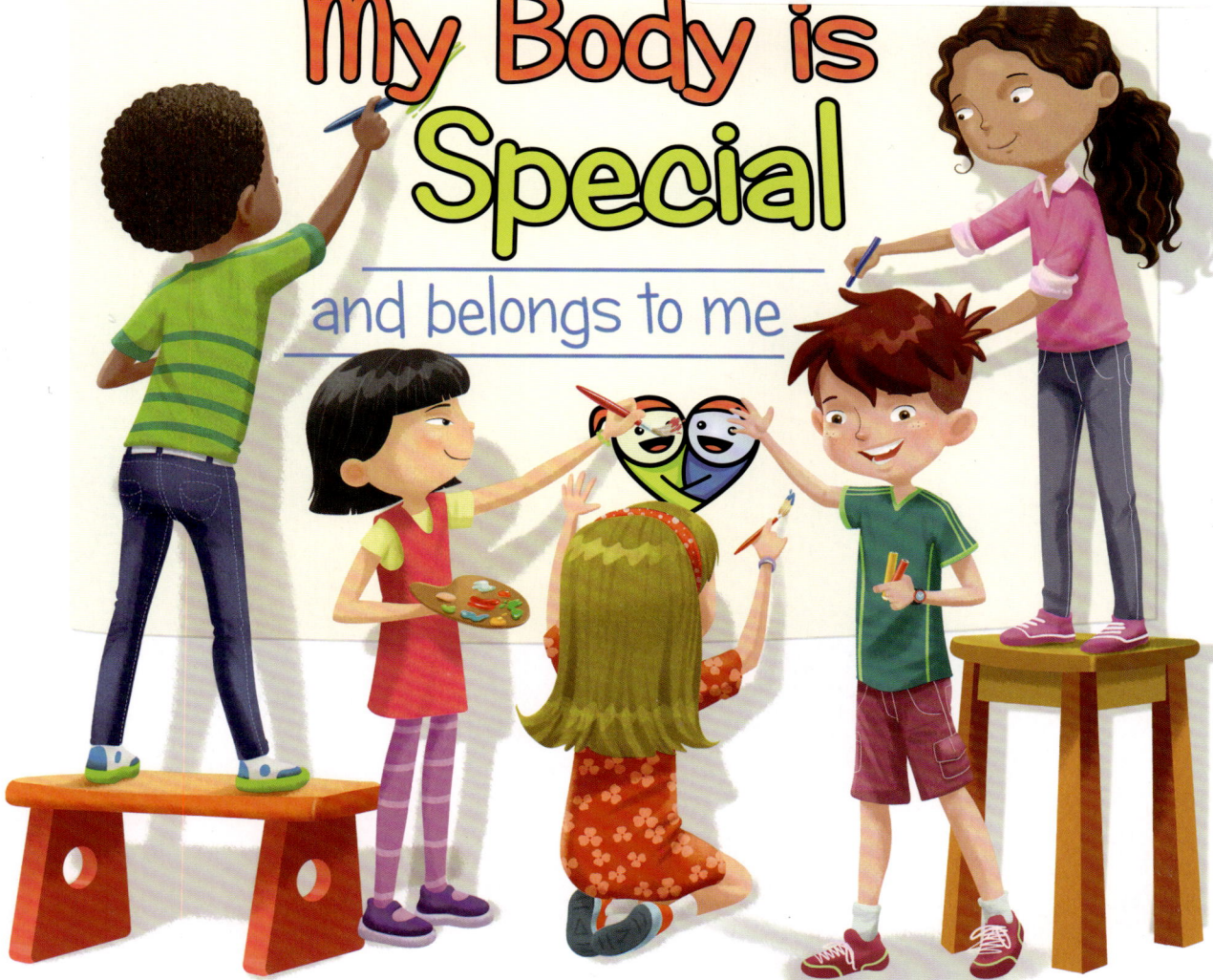

KidSafe
FOUNDATION
Empowered Children Become Powerful Adults

Cherie Benjoseph, LCSW • Sally Berenzweig, MEd, MA

The information provided in this book is designed to provide helpful information on the subjects discussed. This book is not intended to replace the advice or treatment by health care professionals.

KidSafe
FOUNDATION
Empowered Children Become Powerful Adults

www.KidSafeFoundation.org

ISBN: 978-0-9989529-5-6

Design and illustration by AQ Creative Lab
Printed in the United States by Micro Printing

2019 Edition

To Parents Everywhere

💟 for raising safe and smart kids

💟 for empowering yourselves with personal safety knowledge

💟 for teaching your children that they are valued and loved

💟 for being the approachable parent

This Book Is For You And Your Children

From The KidSafe Foundation

Building strong, resilient families and safer communities

Erin Merryn, on a mission to bring mandated education to children across the United States, shares why this book is essential to all families.

Growing up in school each year I was educated with my classmates on tornado drills, fire drills, bus drills, stranger danger, and learned the eight ways to say no to drugs. As a child I never had to use any of these skills in an emergency. Where was the drill on how to escape a child molester? Where was the lesson plan on safe touches, and safe secrets? It never came. I was never educated that my body is special and belongs to me. I was sexually abused starting at age 6. I was confused and scared.

I was displaying all the signs of an abused child, yet nobody ever asked the simple questions, *"Does anyone make you feel uncomfortable?" "Has someone hurt you?" "Do you have any secrets with anyone?"* There were many safe adults in my life, but they failed to give me the message, *"My body is special and belongs to me. I am in charge of my body as you can see."* Had this book existed when I was a child —and been read to me— it would have empowered me to tell my story and could have saved me years of sexual abuse. These pages could have saved my childhood and given me a voice. Imagine for a moment if this book were in the hands of my parents, teachers, social workers, and pediatricians reading it to the once six-year-old that I was.

Erin Merryn is author of *Stolen Innocence, Living for Today,* and *An Unimaginable Act*. She is an activist against child sexual abuse and founder of Erin's Law, which requires public schools to teach children personal body safety. She has appeared on Oprah, CNN, Good Morning America and has been featured in Time Magazine, Cosmo Girl, and numerous others. Learn more at *erinslaw.org*.

KidSafe FOUNDATION
Empowered Children Become Powerful Adults

A Message from KidSafe to Grown-Ups

The key to keeping children safe is to empower families, children and their grown-ups, with skills and knowledge to talk about personal safety.

The *My Body is Special and Belongs to Me!* book is a perfect place to start. It speaks to children and to their grown-ups about body boundaries. Reading this book together helps with listening to and understanding one's feelings, empowering children to know they can access help, and setting the groundwork for teaching consent. Talking with our children about personal safety is a natural part of everyday parenting.

There are tips on how to use this book on page 27. We recommend you take a few minutes to read through to the end before you share with your child to get the most out of your experience.

The Parent's Place section is online at *www.KidSafeFoundation.org*. We welcome you to visit and #askKidSafe.

Working together to keep **KidSafe**,

The **KidSafe** Family

Thank you for joining us on the **KidSafe** mission to teach personal safety to children and their grown-ups to build strong, resilient families and safer communities.

To find out more about **KidSafe** and the authors visit
www.KidSafeFoundation.org

I am KidSafe smart and I have a lot to share about keeping our bodies safe and treating ourselves with love and care.

Because My Body is Special and belongs to me. I am in charge of my body, as you will see!

I will share many things about what to do to help keep your body safe and take good care of you.
As you read this book, you will see kids who listen to their Safety Voice, just like me!

When you listen to your Safety Voice and think about how a touch feels inside, you can use those feelings as your Safe and Unsafe touch guide.

So think about how many
times we are touched
throughout the day.
We know a touch is Safe
when we feel this way:
Happy, cozy, and
comfortable as can be.
A touch that feels this way
is a Safe touch to me.

When my friend holds my hand, it is a Safe touch to me.
Because I feel warm, comfy, and as joyful as can be.

I love when my Mom or Dad tucks me in at night.
A kiss on my forehead and I feel everything is alright.

When my teacher pats me on the back
and says "You are so smart,"
I feel proud and special
with a cozy feeling in my heart.

But sometimes a touch can make you feel bad. Being pushed on the playground might make you feel sad.

If my hair was pulled,
it would really hurt me.
I would feel mad and uncomfortable;
an unsafe touch it would be.

My sister likes to tickle me,
and it can feel real good.
I feel special and loved;
just like a brother and sister
should.

That was
too much,
Sis.

When I want her to stop
because it no longer feels good,
I use my Safety Voice to stop her
and I hope that she would.

I like to get hugs, then sometimes I don't.
I like to give kisses, but sometimes I won't.
Come give your uncle a hug!
No thanks. How about a high five?
My parents told me I can say "No" to a touch. Even from someone I know and love so much.
Because My Body Is Special and belongs to me. I am in charge of my body, as you can see!

Taking care of my body is something I am learning to do. Washing and dressing are now my jobs, too.

You can learn to take care of your body, just like me. Our bodies are special, as you can see.

I have private parts that belong just to me.
They are under my bathing suit,
but I won't let you see.

You have private parts
that are special, too.
No one should touch them —
they are meant just for YOU!

But if I have a rash or my private parts
don't feel like they should,
my parents take me to the Doctor and
if she needs to see them, she could.

Because My Body Is Special and belongs to me.
I am in charge of my body, as you can see!

If you get a touch on your private parts,
and you feel weird and confused in your heart,
try to use your Safety Voice as fast as you can.
Go tell a grown-up, they will understand.

Great job Reporting! I am so glad you came to tell me.

It is never your fault if you get a touch that is confusing to you. Make sure you tell a grown-up, they will know what to do.

If someone gives you a touch and says, "Now don't you tell." Don't keep that touch a secret; tell an adult you know well.
Don't tell your parents, this is our special secret.
If someone gives you a present and says, "Keep it a secret between you and me," Tell a grown-up you trust *immediately!*

Your Circle of Safe Adults is where you should go.
When you have a problem, these adults need to know.

Don't keep it inside, share what is bothering you.
So you can get the help you need and stay safe, too!

Most touches make us feel comfortable, special, and safe.
Getting a hug from someone you love can make you feel great.

So now say these words with me.
Believe it, and it will come to be:

MY BODY IS SPECIAL AND BELONGS TO ME.
I AM IN CHARGE OF MY BODY, AS YOU CAN SEE!

So as we end this book
I will go give a hug
to someone who is special,
to someone I love.

You can give someone you love a hug, too.
It's always your choice, because your body belongs to YOU!

Draw a picture of three adults you trust and could talk to about anything.
Write their names next to their picture.

Circle of Safe Adults

How to Get the Most Out of this book

Before reading with your child:

Read the book yourself cover to cover. This will give you the opportunity to familiarize yourself with the content and feel of the book.

Read the children's pages out loud to get comfortable with the rhyming.

Share the book with any other significant grown-ups in your child's life.

During reading with your child:

During the first reading let your child and yourself enjoy the book as is. Children find this a comforting book and will ask for it to be read over and over.

Monitor your child's understanding by asking questions about the illustrations. Some examples: "Can you point to where the safe touch is in the picture?" "What is the child doing in the picture?"

Expand the learning by asking further questions: "How do you think the little boy is feeling in this picture? How do you know?" "What is a safe touch for you?" "Who are some people in your Circle of Safe Adults?" "What do you think the girl in the picture should do?" "Does the little girl have to hug her uncle? Why or Why not?"

After reading with your child:

Integrate the key KidSafe Language of Safety words into your everyday parenting. (Safety Voice, Circle of Safe Adults, Good Secret/Bad Secret, Safe Touch/Unsafe Touch). And of course – My Body is Special and Belongs to Me.

Teach your children the proper names for their private parts.

Encourage your child to use their Safety Voice.

Label everyday 'touches'. For example: "When your brother held your hand as we crossed the street was that a safe touch or an unsafe touch for you?" or "When your sister hit you in the car was that a safe touch or an unsafe touch?" "What were you feeling?"

Have your child draw a picture of their Circle of Safe Adults. You can find a sample to download at www.KidSafeFoundation.org

Parent's Place

Welcome to the wonderful world of talking with your children about their personal safety.

This book provides you with a positive and empowering story to read with your children to teach them about their personal safety. Together you will open a comfortable conversation with children about:

- body boundaries
- listening to their feelings
- using their safety voice
- good and bad secrets
- trusted grown-ups and much more.

Our goal is to raise safe and smart independent kids who know their personal boundaries, have open communication with their trusted grown-ups and know how to access help when needed.

We want all adults who are sharing this book with children to teach personal safety from a place of empowerment, not from a place of fear. Every child finds comfort in knowing he or she can go to a safe grown-up who will listen and help.

There is much to talk about on this journey of Personal Safety. Visit us at www.KidSafeFoundation.org, and find helpful answers to some of your parenting questions.

- When should I start teaching my child the proper names for their private parts?
- Is it okay to let my child go on sleep overs?
- What do I do when my child won't give a kiss or hug to my relatives?
- How can I teach my child more about safe touch and unsafe touch?
- Who are the people who harm kids?
- How do I vet a babysitter?

To find more KidSafe information and to #askKidSafe visit us at www.KidSafeFoundation.org